I0490831

1 Hour Payday:

The Ultimate

Guide to Making

Money Quickly

By

Margo Cale

TABLE of CONTENTS

Introduction:

Are you tired of living pay check to pay check and struggling to make ends meet? Do you wish you could have a little extra cash in your pocket without having to wait weeks or months for your next paycheck? If so, you're not alone. Many people today are looking for ways to make money quickly, and that's exactly what this book is all about.

In "1 Hour Payday: The Ultimate Guide to Making Money Quickly," we'll explore a variety of strategies and techniques that you can use to start earning extra cash right away. Whether you're looking to supplement your income, save up for a big purchase, or pay off debt, the tips and insights in this book will help you achieve your financial goals.

In the following chapters, we'll cover everything from freelancing and online entrepreneurship to investing in stocks and cryptocurrencies. We'll also explore ways to make money through social media, selling products online, and even renting out your property. No matter what your skills or interests may be, there's something in this book for everyone.

So, if you're ready to take control of your finances and start earning more money today, let's get started!

Chapter 1: The Power of Quick Cash

When it comes to making money quickly, there's a certain power that comes with it. Being able to earn extra cash on short notice can give you a sense of freedom and control over your finances that you may not have had before. But what exactly is quick cash, and why is it so valuable?

Quick cash refers to any money that you can earn in a short amount of time, usually within a day or two. This type of income can come from a variety of sources, including freelance work, odd jobs, selling unwanted items, and more. The key to earning quick cash is being resourceful and finding opportunities where others might not see them.

There are many benefits to having access to quick cash. For one, it can help you cover unexpected expenses that may arise, such as car repairs or medical bills. It can also provide a cushion during lean times when your regular income may not be enough to cover your expenses. And of course, having extra cash on hand can also give you more freedom and flexibility in your day-to-day life.

In the following chapters, we'll explore a variety of strategies and techniques for earning quick cash, no matter what your skills or interests may be. Whether you're looking to make a little extra money on the side or launch a full-fledged entrepreneurial venture, we've got you covered. So let's dive in and start exploring the many ways you can start earning

quick cash today.

Chapter 2: Identifying Your Income Sources

Before you can start earning quick cash, it's important to identify where your income is coming from. This means taking a close look at your current job or career, as well as any side hustles or freelance work you may be doing.

Start by examining your current job or career. Are there opportunities for overtime or extra shifts that you can take advantage of? Can you negotiate a raise or bonus with your employer? Are there any opportunities for advancement or promotion within your company? These are all potential ways to increase your income in the short term.

Next, think about any skills or talents you may have that could be monetized. Are you good at writing or graphic design? Do you have experience in photography or video production? Are you a skilled handyman or DIY enthusiast? These are all potential sources of income that you can leverage to make quick cash.

You can also consider taking on freelance work or short-term gigs through platforms like Upwork, Fiverr, or TaskRabbit. These platforms connect freelancers with clients who need their services, and can be a great way to earn extra cash on your own schedule.

Finally, think about any assets you may have that could be rented or sold. Do you have a spare room in your home that you could rent out on Airbnb? Do you have a car that you could rent out on Turo? Do you have any unwanted items that you could sell on eBay or Facebook Marketplace? These are all potential sources of income that can help you earn quick cash.

By identifying your income sources, you'll be able to focus your efforts on the areas where you're most likely to earn quick cash. In the following chapters, we'll explore each of these income sources in more detail, and provide tips and strategies for maximizing your earnings in each area.

Chapter 3: Maximizing Your Earnings at Your Job

If you're looking to earn quick cash, one of the easiest places to start is with your current job. Here are some strategies for maximizing your earnings at work:

Take on overtime or extra shifts: If your employer offers overtime or extra shifts, consider taking them on to earn extra income. This can be a great way to earn more money without having to take on a second job.

Negotiate a raise or bonus: If you feel like you deserve to be paid more for the work you're doing, consider negotiating a raise or bonus with your employer. Make a case for why you deserve more money and be prepared to provide examples of your accomplishments and contributions to the company.

Look for opportunities for advancement: If you're interested in advancing your career, look for opportunities to take on more responsibility or move up within your company. This can not only lead to higher earnings in the long term, but it can also help you earn more money in the short term through promotions or bonuses.

Sell back vacation or sick time: Some employers allow their employees to sell back their unused vacation or sick time for extra income. Check with your HR department to see if this is an option for you.

Take advantage of employee discounts or perks: Many employers offer employee discounts or perks, such as discounted gym memberships, free meals, or even company-sponsored events. Take advantage of these benefits to save money and reduce your expenses.

By taking these steps, you can maximize your earnings at your current job and earn quick cash without having to take on a second job or side hustle. In the next chapter, we'll explore how you can leverage your skills and talents to earn

additional income outside of your regular job.

Chapter 4: Leveraging Your Skills and Talents

If you have skills or talents that can be monetized, there are many ways to earn quick cash outside of your regular job. Here are some strategies for leveraging your skills and talents to earn additional income:

Freelancing: If you have skills in writing, graphic design, web development, or other areas, consider freelancing on platforms like Upwork, Fiverr, or Freelancer. You can offer your services to clients around the world and earn money on your own schedule.

Photography or videography: If you have a talent for photography or videography, consider offering your services for events, weddings, or even stock photography websites like Shutterstock or Getty Images.

DIY or handyman services: If you're handy around the house, consider offering your services for small home repairs, installations, or DIY projects. You can advertise your services on Craigslist, Facebook Marketplace, or TaskRabbit.

Personal training or coaching: If you're a fitness enthusiast or have experience in coaching or mentoring, consider offering your services as a personal trainer or coach. You can work with clients one-on-one or even offer online coaching services.

Teaching or tutoring: If you have expertise in a particular subject, consider offering your services as a tutor or teacher. You can advertise your services on websites like Tutor.com or even offer your services locally.

By leveraging your skills and talents, you can earn quick cash on your own schedule and on your own terms. In the next chapter, we'll explore how you can earn additional income by renting or selling assets you already own.

Chapter 5: Renting or Selling Your Assets

If you own assets that are not being used, you can rent or sell them to earn quick cash. Here are some ideas for renting or selling assets you already own:

Rent out your spare room: If you have a spare room in your house or apartment, consider renting it out on Airbnb or other short-term rental platforms. This can be a great way to earn extra income, especially if you live in a desirable location.

Rent out your car: If you have a car that's not being used all the time, consider renting it out on platforms like Turo or Getaround. This can be a great way to earn money while your car is just sitting in your driveway.

Sell unwanted items: If you have unwanted items lying around your house, consider selling them on platforms like eBay or Craigslist. This can be a great way to earn some quick cash while decluttering your home.

Rent out equipment: If you have equipment that's not being used all the time, consider renting it out to others. For example, if you have a camera or video equipment, you can rent it out to others for events or projects.

Rent out outdoor space: If you have outdoor space like a backyard or garage, consider renting it out to others for storage or events. You can advertise your space on platforms like Spacer or Store at My House.

By renting or selling assets you already own, you can earn quick cash without having to take on additional work or invest in new ventures. In the next chapter, we'll explore how you can take advantage of the gig economy to earn quick cash on your own schedule.

Chapter 6: Making Money in the Gig Economy

The gig economy has made it easier than ever to earn quick cash on your own schedule. Here are some ideas for making money in the gig economy:

Delivery services: With the rise of food delivery and courier services like UberEats, DoorDash, and Postmates, it's easier than ever to earn money delivering food or packages. All you need is a car or bike, a smartphone, and some free time.

Task-based platforms: Task-based platforms like TaskRabbit or Airtasker allow you to earn money doing a variety of tasks for others, such as cleaning, moving, or even assembling furniture.

Pet-sitting or dog-walking: If you love animals, consider offering your services as a pet-sitter or dog-walker. You can advertise your services on platforms like Rover or Wag.

Online surveys: There are many websites that will pay you for taking online surveys, such as Swagbucks or Survey Junkie. While you won't get rich doing this, it can be a quick and easy way to earn some extra cash in your spare time.

Online freelancing: There are many freelancing platforms like Freelancer or Upwork where you can offer your skills and services to clients around the world. You can earn money on your own schedule and work from anywhere.

By taking advantage of the gig economy, you can earn quick cash on your own schedule and without having to commit to a full-time job. However, it's important to remember that many of these opportunities are not full-time or consistent, so it's important to have a backup plan and not rely solely on the gig economy for income.

Chapter 7: Investing for Quick Cash

Investing can be a great way to earn quick cash, but it also comes with risks. Here are some ideas for investing for quick cash:

Day trading: Day trading involves buying and selling stocks within the same trading day in order to earn quick profits. This can be a risky strategy, as it requires a lot of knowledge and skill to be successful.

Peer-to-peer lending: Peer-to-peer lending platforms like LendingClub or Prosper allow you to lend money to others and earn interest on your investment. While this can be a good way to earn steady income, it also comes with risks if borrowers' default on their loans.

Real estate: Real estate investing can be a great way to earn passive income, especially if you buy rental properties. You can also invest in real estate investment trusts (REITs) or real estate crowdfunding platforms like Fundrise or RealtyMogul.

Cryptocurrency: Cryptocurrency like Bitcoin or Ethereum can be a volatile investment, but it's also one that can offer quick returns. However, it's important to do your research and understand the risks before investing in cryptocurrency.

High-yield savings accounts or CDs: While not as high-risk or high-reward as other investment strategies, high-yield savings accounts or certificates of deposit (CDs) can offer steady, guaranteed returns on your investment.

Investing can be a great way to earn quick cash, but it's important to understand the risks and do your research before making any investments. It's also important to have a diversified investment portfolio and not rely solely on one strategy for income.

Chapter 8: Starting a Side Business

Starting a side business can be a great way to earn quick cash, especially if you have a particular skill or passion. Here are some ideas for starting a side business:

Freelance services: If you have a particular skill like graphic design, writing, or web development, you can offer your services as a freelancer. You can advertise your services on platforms like Fiverr or Upwork, or create your own website and market your services directly to clients.

Etsy or Amazon Handmade: If you're crafty, consider selling your handmade items on Etsy or Amazon Handmade. This can be a great way to turn your hobby into a profitable side business.

Airbnb: If you have extra space in your home, consider renting it out on Airbnb. This can be a great way to earn extra money, especially if you live in a popular tourist destination.

Tutoring or teaching: If you have a particular skill or subject knowledge, consider offering your services as a tutor or teacher. You can advertise your services online or through local schools and tutoring centers.

Photography: If you have a talent for photography, consider offering your services for events like weddings or family portraits. You can also sell your photos online through platforms like Shutterstock or Adobe Stock.

Starting a side business can be a great way to earn extra income, but it's important to remember that it requires time and effort to get started and be successful. It's important to do your research, develop a solid business plan, and be prepared to invest time and money into your business.

Chapter 9: Selling Unwanted Items

One of the quickest ways to earn cash is by selling items you no longer need or want. Here are some ideas for selling unwanted items:

Online marketplaces: Websites like eBay, Amazon, or Craigslist can be great platforms to sell unwanted items. You can list anything from clothes to electronics and reach a wide audience of potential buyers.

Consignment stores: Consignment stores like Plato's Closet or Buffalo Exchange will pay you cash for gently used clothing and accessories.

Garage sales: Hosting a garage sale can be a great way to get rid of unwanted items and earn quick cash. You can advertise your sale on local classifieds or social media.

Pawn shops: If you have valuable items like jewelry or electronics, consider selling them to a pawn shop. They will offer you cash on the spot for your items.

Sell on social media: Facebook Marketplace or Instagram can be great platforms to sell unwanted items to people in your community. You can join local buy and sell groups and post pictures of your items for sale.

Selling unwanted items can be a great way to earn quick cash, especially if you have a lot of items to sell. It's important to research the value of your items and price them competitively, as well as taking good photos and writing accurate descriptions to attract potential buyers.

Chapter 10: Taking on Odd Jobs

Taking on odd jobs can be a great way to earn quick cash, especially if you're willing to do a variety of tasks. Here are some ideas for taking on odd jobs:

Task-based apps: There are several apps like TaskRabbit, Thumbtack, or Gigwalk that connect people with odd jobs to people who are willing to do them. These apps can offer a wide variety of tasks, from cleaning to handyman work to personal shopping.

Yard work: If you have a green thumb, consider offering your services for yard work like mowing lawns, trimming bushes, or planting flowers.

Pet care: If you love animals, consider offering pet care services like dog walking, pet sitting, or grooming.

Moving or delivery services: If you have a truck or van, consider offering moving or delivery services for people in your community.

Event staffing: Many companies hire temporary event staff for things like weddings, concerts, or festivals. You can often find these jobs through staffing agencies or online job boards.

Taking on odd jobs can be a great way to earn extra cash, but it's important to remember that these jobs can often be physically demanding and may require specific skills or qualifications. It's important to assess your own abilities and interests before taking on any odd jobs, and to always prioritize your safety and well-being while working.

Chapter 11: Renting Out Your Space

If you have extra space in your home or apartment, renting it out can be a great way to earn some extra cash. Here are some ideas for renting out your space:

Airbnb: If you have a spare bedroom or an entire apartment or house, consider renting it out on Airbnb. You can set your own price and availability, and Airbnb handles all the booking and payment details.

Storage space: If you have a garage or extra room that isn't being used, consider renting it out as storage space. There are websites like StoreAtMyHouse that connect people in need of storage space with people who have extra space to rent.

Parking space: If you have an extra parking space or garage, consider renting it out to someone in need of parking. Websites like JustPark or Parkhound connect people in need of parking with people who have space to rent.

Event space: If you have a large backyard or a spacious living area, consider renting it out as an event space for things like weddings, parties, or photo shoots. Websites like Peerspace or Splacer connect people in need of event spaces with people who have space to rent.

Renting out your space can be a great way to earn some extra cash, but it's important to remember that it comes with some risks. It's important to thoroughly screen potential renters and to have a solid rental agreement in place to protect yourself and your property.

Chapter 12: Freelancing and Consulting

If you have specific skills or expertise, freelancing or consulting can be a great way to earn extra money. Here are some ideas for freelancing or consulting:

Writing or editing: If you have strong writing or editing skills, consider offering your services to clients in need of content for their websites, blogs, or marketing materials.

Graphic design: If you have experience with graphic design, consider offering your services for things like logo design, website design, or print materials.

Social media management: If you're a social media whiz, consider offering your services to small businesses in need of help managing their social media presence.

Web development: If you have experience with web development, consider offering your services for website creation or updates.

Consulting: If you have expertise in a specific industry or field, consider offering consulting services to businesses or individuals in need of advice or guidance.

Freelancing and consulting can be a great way to earn extra money, but it's important to remember that you'll need to market yourself and find clients on your own. It's also important to set clear expectations and boundaries with clients to ensure that you're compensated fairly for your work.

Chapter 13: Selling Online

The rise of e-commerce has made it easier than ever to sell products online. Here are some ideas for selling online:

Etsy: If you're a crafty person or have a talent for creating handmade items, consider selling them on Etsy. Etsy is a popular online marketplace for handmade and vintage goods.

eBay: eBay is one of the oldest and most well-known online marketplaces. You can sell almost anything on eBay, from used clothing to vintage collectibles.

Amazon: If you have a product to sell, consider listing it on Amazon. Amazon is the largest online retailer in the world, and listing your product on their site can give you access to a large customer base.

Shopify: If you want to create your own online store, consider using Shopify. Shopify is an e-commerce platform that allows you to create your own online store and sell your products directly to customers.

Selling online can be a great way to earn extra money, but it's important to remember that you'll need to market your products and manage your online presence to be successful. You'll also need to handle things like shipping and customer service, so be prepared to put in some work.

Chapter 14: Investing

Investing can be a great way to earn passive income and grow your wealth over time. Here are some investment options to consider:

Stocks: Investing in stocks is one of the most popular ways to grow your wealth. You can purchase stocks through a brokerage account and potentially earn a return on your investment as the stock price increases.

Bonds: Bonds are a type of investment that allow you to lend money to a company or government in exchange for interest payments. Bonds can be a good option for those who want a more stable investment with less risk.

Real estate: Investing in real estate can be a good way to earn passive income through rental properties or to make a profit by buying and flipping properties.

Mutual funds: Mutual funds allow you to invest in a diverse portfolio of stocks and bonds, which can help to mitigate risk and potentially earn a higher return on your investment.

Index funds: Index funds are similar to mutual funds, but they track a specific index, such as the S&P 500. Index funds can be a good option for those who want to invest in the stock market but don't want to pick individual stocks.

Investing can be a complex topic, so it's important to do your research and speak with a financial advisor before making any investment decisions. However, with the right strategy and knowledge, investing can be a great way to build long-term wealth.

Chapter 15: Freelancing

Freelancing is becoming an increasingly popular way to earn income, especially with the rise of the gig economy. Here are some tips for freelancing:

Determine your skills: Freelancing requires a specific set of skills, so it's important to determine what you can offer to potential clients. This could include writing, graphic design, web development, social media management, or many other skills.

Build your portfolio: Once you've determined your skills, it's important to build a portfolio of your work. This will help you showcase your abilities to potential clients and can help you stand out in a competitive market.

Set your rates: Freelancers often charge by the hour or by the project. It's important to set your rates based on your experience and the value you bring to clients.

Market yourself: Freelancing requires you to market yourself and find clients. You can do this through social media, job boards, and networking events.

Manage your time: As a freelancer, you'll need to manage your own time and prioritize your work. This can be a challenge, but it's important to maintain a balance between work and personal life.

Freelancing can be a great way to earn income and have more control over your career. However, it's important to remember that freelancing can also be unpredictable and requires self-discipline and hard work.

Conclusion:

In conclusion, earning a living can be a challenging and complex process, but there are many strategies and tips you can use to make it easier. By exploring different career options, building your skills, networking, and managing your finances, you can set yourself up for success and achieve your financial goals.

It's important to remember that everyone's journey is unique, and there's no one-size-fits-all approach to earning a living. However, with perseverance and a willingness to learn and adapt, you can create a fulfilling and financially stable life for yourself.

We hope this book has provided you with valuable insights and practical tips for earning a living. Whether you're just starting out in your career or looking to make a change, we wish you the best of luck on your journey.